Tyne & Wear

Edited By Donna Samworth

First published in Great Britain in 2018 by:

Young Writers
Remus House
Coltsfoot Drive
Peterborough
PE2 9BF
Telephone: 01733 890066
Website: www.youngwriters.co.uk

All Rights Reserved
Book Design by Ashley Janson
© Copyright Contributors 2017
SB ISBN 978-1-78896-042-7
Printed and bound in the UK by BookPrintingUK
Website: www.bookprintinguk.com
YB0343G

FOREWORD

Welcome Reader, to *Rhymecraft - Tyne & Wear*.

Among these pages you will find a whole host of poetic gems, built from the ground up by some wonderful young minds. Included are a variety of poetic styles, from amazing acrostics to creative cinquains, from dazzling diamantes to fascinating free verse.

Here at Young Writers our objective has always been to help children discover the joys of poetry and creative writing. Few things are more encouraging for the aspiring writer than seeing their own work in print. We are proud that our anthologies are able to give young authors this unique sense of confidence and pride in their abilities as well as letting their poetry reach new audiences.

The editing process was a tough but rewarding one that allowed us to gain an insight into the blooming creativity of today's primary school pupils. I hope you find as much enjoyment and inspiration in the following poetry as I have, so much so that you pick up a pen and get writing!

Donna Samworth

CONTENTS

Argyle House School, Sunderland

Scarlett Elizabeth Reavley (8)	1
Max Gray Westall (10)	2
Keziah Zoe Harris (10)	3
Harry Hutcheon (8)	4

Diamond Hall Junior School, Millfield

Georgia Matthews (10)	5
Poppy Louise Dawson (10)	6
Samantha Jane Ward (10)	8
Ellie Hunter (10)	10
Christopher Kose (10)	12
Deborah Aisida (10)	13
Leah June Docherty (11)	14
Nathan Thomas Kennedy (11)	15
Shujath Zaman (10)	16
Mia Robson (10)	17
Lauren Stephenson (10)	18
Summer Loughton (10)	19
Haadi Abdul (10)	20
Jeremiah Ortega Fanggo (10)	21
Chloe Thompson (10)	22
Muhammad Fauzaan Abdullah (10)	23

Rickleton Primary School, Washington

Matthew Rutherford (9)	24
Tess Guthrie (9)	26
Oliver Hay (9)	27
Sasha Kate Latimer (10)	28
Jenna Everett (10)	30
Amy Bell (10)	32

Matthew Jones (9)	34
Rajan Singh (9)	35
Jack Andrew Lawson (9)	36
Aimee Mae Harrison (10)	38
Nathan Rajeev (10)	39
Damarah Middlemas (9)	40
Lincoln Adamson (9)	41
Ella McNally (9)	42
Ellie Grace Bramley (9)	43
Lily-May Gould (9)	44
Amelia Ava Goodwin (9)	45
Adam Davies (9)	46
Louis Cutler (9)	47
Keerat Singh Uppal (9)	48
Adam Kean (9)	49
Lydia Laidler (10)	50
Daniel Robson (10)	51
Emily Pauc (9)	52
Cadon Howarth (10)	53
Mark Patterson (10)	54
Elliot Jordan Curry (10)	55
Imogen Lucy Moat (9)	56
Evie Grace Shield (10)	57
Grace Winter (11)	58
Jasmine Dhillon (9)	59
James Michael Southern (9)	60
Brooke Northey (9)	61
Cuan Snell (10)	62
Jake Lish (9)	63
Arin Cohan (9)	64
Amrit Kaur Dulai (10)	65
Casey James Ritchie (10)	66
Edie Rebecca Macbeth (9)	67
Dixie Martha Baker (10)	68
Kayleigh Rafferty (10)	69

Emily Bradney (9)	70
Anna Jayne Whitfield (9)	71
Elisha Turnbull (11)	72
Logan Green (10)	73
Rebecca Marsh (10)	74
Nathan Alcock (9)	75
Max Burlison (10)	76
Priya Seren Dhindsa (9)	77
Sophie Dunn (9)	78
Callum Morrison (11)	79
Grace Elizabeth Hewitt (11)	80
Harriet Georgia Dunn (9)	81
Amelia Isabelle Lowden (10)	82
Jon-James Robert Ware (10)	83
Charlie William Miller (11)	84
Ben Hovvels (9)	85
Zachary Wheat (10)	86
Innes Batey (10)	87
Nathan Olley (10)	88

St Oswald's RC Primary School, South Shields

Caleb Shay Buckingham (8)	89
Harry James Wales (8)	90
Joe Steel (9)	92
Marissa Towns (8)	94
Poppy Grace Melia (9)	95
Ruby Calvert (8)	96
Toby Male (8)	97
Rebecca Louise Robson (8)	98
Stevey Louise Burrough (8)	99
Rebecca Stonehouse (8)	100
Oliver Stirling Welsh (8)	101
Noah Robinson (8)	102

Trinity Academy - Deneview, South Gosforth

Harley Celino (9)	103
Bradley Walters (10)	104
Llayton Wharton (10)	106
Joshua Hunter (9)	107
Alfie Watts (7)	108

Nathan Johnston (9)	109
Leighton Turnbull (9)	110
Kai Forrest (7)	111
Elisha Collinson (9)	112
Shane Mills (7)	113
Robert Hurst (8)	114
Charlie Scott (7)	115
Caine Campbell (9)	116
Louis Maughan (8)	117

Wellfield Middle School, Whitley Bay

Robert William McGuffog (9)	118
Katie Coventry (10)	120
Charlie Pirie (9)	122
Oliver Wood (10)	124
Emily Morton (9)	126
Amelia McClurry (9)	127
Ewan Sumby (9)	128
Vaughn Rhodes (9)	130
Niamh Caitlin Nicholson (9)	131
Eloise Conway (9)	132
Lola Fischer (9)	133
Louie Brown (9)	134
Harrison Nisbet (9)	135
Aaron Wood (9)	136
Lucy France (9)	137
Matthew White (9)	138
Oskar Armutcuoglu (9)	139
Maddy Coll (9)	140
Eoin Winder (9)	141
Jake Humphrey (10)	142
Alfie James Ord (10)	143
Daniel Ross (10)	144
Carley Coates (9)	145
Daryl Davison (10)	146
Tyler Ewart (9)	147
Leo Richards (9)	148
Charlie Payne (9)	149
Emily Scott (9)	150
Alfie Robert William Burnip (9)	151
Samuel Birkett (10)	152
Morgan Smith (9)	153

Eva Holly Pattison (9)	154
Harli-Mae Sydney Mawson (9)	155
Dan Moll (9)	156
Rosie Campbell (9)	157
Fraser Potter (9)	158
Ben Vincent (9)	159
Ryan Cain (9)	160
Grant Steven Milburn (9)	161
Thomas Stanley (9)	162
James Worsdale (9)	163
Dylan Robinson (9)	164
Ava Tierney (10)	165
Daniel Browell (10)	166
Luke Mennie (9)	167
Olivia Farrington (9)	168
Carla Filipa Paulino-Goncalves (9)	169
Thomas Sidebotham (9)	170
Sophie Johnson (9)	171
Phoebe Olivia Batchelor (9)	172
Amelia Dodds (9)	173
Max Torre (9)	174
Aimee Cowen (9)	175
Oliver Stoneman (9)	176
Josh Meredith (9)	177
Josh Farrington (9)	178
Ashton Stewart (9)	179

THE POEMS

Surviving At Night!

Surviving at night gives me a fright!
Try as I might, I can't leave my plight.
My weapon in hand, I must make my stand.
This is my land, I will not be unmanned.

Where will those creepers be stalking tonight?
With my newly built house, I know I'll be all right.
But with the resources running low,
it pains me to go!

Avoiding the mobs, I dash to a cave!
I mine and I mine, trying to be brave.
Crushing the stones, I can't hear the noise...
A creeper appears, it wants to destroy!

With a *sizzle* and a *pop*, it explodes with a *bang!*
So it's goodbye for me. Oh dear! Oh dang!

Scarlett Elizabeth Reavley (8)
Argyle House School, Sunderland

Top Tennis

Bing, bang! as I hit the ball
So hard, I think I might fall.
I hit my ace to outer space,
I hit a good backhand slice as I roll the dice.
High ball, it's a smash,
I hit it as fast as a flash.
Bang! I hit my volley so hard.
Two-handed backhand, too easy for me,
I could hit an apple tree.
One more shot of the match,
I won't make it the worst and last.
Bang and I have won, this is my victory!

Max Gray Westall (10)
Argyle House School, Sunderland

Cake

C ake, soft and spongy, always ready to eat.
A ny time at all, cake is my favourite treat.
K eep it in the cupboard, keep it on a tray, keep it on a plate and I will take it away.
E at it for breakfast; eat it for lunch; eat it for dinner; *munch, munch, munch.*

Keziah Zoe Harris (10)
Argyle House School, Sunderland

Steve And The Zombies

F ell over in the forest and got lost,
O nly thing to do was build a house.
R ight away he found bricks and wood
E vening came, so he went to bed.
S teve woke up and saw zombies!
T aking his diamond sword, he killed them all!

Harry Hutcheon (8)
Argyle House School, Sunderland

Soldiers At War!

The soldiers slept under their sacks,
Coughing and shivering as they laid on their backs.
Coming towards them, the rest began to trudge,
The men marched on the fields of blood and sludge.

Bang! Bang! The soldiers were fumbling,
Some were shouting and stumbling.
They fitted their helmets just in time,
The guns they picked up were full of grime.

The flares lit up the cold, misty sky,
Soldiers ahead laid down to die.
The noise made the soldiers deaf to the hoots,
As they marched without their bloodied boots.

Through the misty sky at night,
They could see a thick, green light,
The soldiers were desperate for some glory,
They couldn't wait to get home and tell their story.

Georgia Matthews (10)
Diamond Hall Junior School, Millfield

Full Of Regret

Pew pew!
I can hear the guns shooting
Bang, bang!
I can hear the bombs dropping,
My heart full of regret,
How tragic can this war get?

I and my comrades marched drowsily,
Gas crept up behind us soundlessly.
'Quick, the gas masks, boys!'
Just ignore the background noise.
One of my buddies looks behind him, frowning
And then I see one of my friends drowning.

That event was such a shame,
I no longer speak his name,
Just like any other death, that was his final breath.
The same for tomorrow as well, here in this living hell.

But a sombre sight is the battlefield,
Where all I have is the gun I yield.
With all the memories in my heart,
The war still haunts me in the dark.

Pew pew!
I can still hear the guns shooting,
Bang, bang!
I can still hear the bombs dropping.
My heart full of regret,
How tragic can the war have been?

Poppy Louise Dawson (10)
Diamond Hall Junior School, Millfield

Leaving For War

Our young men all off to serve,
To give our families what they deserve.
Every young soldier going through hell,
Will they live? Time will tell.
Everyone still with fear,
Wondering why they are here.

Going through hell,
No one could tell,
The fear in his eyes,
Wished he'd said his goodbyes.

Young enemy soldiers, just like me,
Probably scared and ready to flee.
A special event in no-man's-land,
A game of football no one planned.
We dropped our weapons and kicked a ball,
With hope, this could be the end for all!

All I wanted to do was get out of those dark, dingy trenches
While the others were climbing those barbed wire fences -
to home!

Samantha Jane Ward (10)
Diamond Hall Junior School, Millfield

Till The End

Knock-kneed,
soldiers in need.
Shells whistling,
nobody listening.

Heart pounding,
bombs landing.
As I clench my fist
I stumble into the trench
and what is this?

Knock-kneed,
soldiers in need.
Shells whistling,
nobody listening.

As I see my fellow mate
who was too late
choking under the green sea.
Suffer! Suffer!

Knock-kneed,
soldiers in need.
Shells whistling,
nobody listening.

As I march onto no-man's-land,
Bang!
I fly through the heavens,
I watch them die!

Knock-kneed,
soldiers in need.
Shells whistling,
nobody listening.

Ellie Hunter (10)
Diamond Hall Junior School, Millfield

Beauty Or A Beast?

A quick blur of brass-brilliant fur, like burnished copper.
Transverse stripes fixed into a mighty body of indomitable courage. Smouldering, amber eyes glaring.
Her colossal forelimbs sprang with coiled energy.
She landed in grace and bared her cruel, curved canines.
The grand base whisked her whip-like tail,
her retractable claws slashed at her prey.

This is the tiger, the apex predator.

A thunderous, full-throated roar boomed.
The royal Bengal beast was triumphant.
She dragged her meal into the murky shadows,
Through the tropical paradise she went,
Until a cave, where her lovely striped cubs slept.

This is the tiger; beauty and the beast.

Christopher Kose (10)
Diamond Hall Junior School, Millfield

Fearless

Dawn breaks the dawn chorus starts
I think of my family
I hope they are not... *Dead!*

Our commander shouts, 'Stand to!'
Then quickly, as quick as lightning,
We all stand straight,
As straight as we can.

The captain walks by,
Looks us up and down,
We all lift our heads
As his fearless eyes stare at us.

We then have our rum ration,
To warm us up,
Warm us up till we are as hot as fire.

Our teeth chatter
In our battered bodies.
My fellow comrades and I
Are afraid of the worst,
But hope for the best.

Deborah Aisida (10)
Diamond Hall Junior School, Millfield

The Drowning Gas

Shaking knees
Like ships tossed upon cloudy seas
A sagging body
With broken bones that finally eased

As he sighed
He thought he might have to say his goodbyes.
'Quick boys, gas! Gas! Gas!'
I immediately put on my mask.

Maybe I was too late
Maybe I had done wrong
But all I could hear was
Screaming... Screaming... Screaming!

My dearest of friends screamed, 'Please God, oh please!'
And then the silence and no one could hear his screams.
He was drowning upon a sea of breeze.

Leah June Docherty (11)
Diamond Hall Junior School, Millfield

This Is War!

Looking around,
The battle scene was harsh,
Bodies lay scattered on the ground,
With the nauseating scent of blood
Surrounding me.

I can hardly see,
For smoke blinds my eyes
And as I look around,
My heart sinks
And fills with sorrow.
I want this battle to end.
Noises of gunfire hurt my eardrums,
Piercing and killing lives.

The images and feelings
Scar me for life.
This is the place of death
And I try hard to keep hope.
This is war!

Nathan Thomas Kennedy (11)
Diamond Hall Junior School, Millfield

The Pain

There is always bloodshed on the ground.
We are mostly sniffed out by bloodhounds.
This is pain.
The greatest pain.

Feeling pain from our boots,
Being killed for looks.
Always feeling like slime,
Our blood dripping like slime.
This is the pain.

There is always bloodshed on the ground.
We are mostly sniffed out by bloodhounds.
This is pain.
The greatest pain.

We're knock-kneed,
And we are drunk with fatigue.

Shujath Zaman (10)
Diamond Hall Junior School, Millfield

Honestum Est Pro Patria Mori?

When I couldn't escape the hive,
I'd done everything to survive,
Yet I could no longer stay alive,
Honestum est pro patria Mori?

I escaped the ship when it sank,
And dodged an attack from a tank.
I tasted the rum that I drank,
Honestum est pro patria Mori?

I didn't expect to get shot,
I was cold where I was once hot.
The blood was not starting to clot,
Honestum est pro patria Mori?

Mia Robson (10)
Diamond Hall Junior School, Millfield

A Suicide

A suicide in the trenches,
Is such a horrible thing to do.
You pull the trigger,
There's nothing left of you,
The gun pulls and, *boom!*

On a stormy day,
A devastating day,
To end your life,
You'll never live again.

You fall on the ground,
Not making the sound,
Nobody knows why you have to die.

I'm so sorry,
I will see you again,
Don't you worry.

Lauren Stephenson (10)
Diamond Hall Junior School, Millfield

Trench Days

Inside this trench
We have no bench.
A stench
That we must clench.

These trench days
Will give us the greys.
We live without charm
As our captain is our alarm.
We live in glory,
Whilst our lives are quite gory.

Overseas it's great
Whilst over here it's fate
I can see a mighty flare
Someone will stare
As these trench days
May have something to say.

Summer Loughton (10)
Diamond Hall Junior School, Millfield

Untitled

As I woke up in another disastrous day,
Something worse happening every day.
So many die,
So many cry.

My poor fellow's foot was numb,
The sun was so hot it made a flood.
My best fellow was shot,
He could see the light coming up at him.

As I took cover,
I saw my friend calling for his mother.
I was the same, very afraid.
I was wondering how long I would live...

Haadi Abdul (10)
Diamond Hall Junior School, Millfield

Bombs

Bombs are not calm, however they are strong
People who are scared of them are not doing wrong.
They are as loud as a howl
But don't sound like a growl.

The war is very scary
Especially with bombs
There are shells on the battlefield.
Marks on the land.

Flares every day
Bombs are just scary
Something to be afraid of.

Jeremiah Ortega Fanggo (10)
Diamond Hall Junior School, Millfield

Untitled

Death leaves hearts broken that no one can heal.
But the memory the heart keeps, it cannot steal.
The memory will start to fade
But the soldier's friends just prayed.
Everyone sat on a pile of bricks
Near some dust and sticks.
'I hope he is okay!'

Chloe Thompson (10)
Diamond Hall Junior School, Millfield

Untitled

Scared of war,
Bored and sore,
Ran on the shoreline,
Dirty trenches,
Tinned food,
Rats everywhere,
Fall in despair,
One set of clothes,
Man-made walls,
Horrible war.

Muhammad Fauzaan Abdullah (10)
Diamond Hall Junior School, Millfield

Seasons

Spring
- **S** pring is a time of rebirth
- **P** urple crocuses grow from the earth
- **R** ainy days through April and May
- **I** n the fields, lambs frolic and play
- **N** ew chicks hatch, they chirp and cheep
- **G** roups of hedgehogs awake from their sleep.

Summer
- **S** ummer is a happy time
- **U** nderneath the bright sunshine
- **M** assive ice cream sundaes
- **M** any happy fun days
- **E** veryone splashing in the sea
- **R** elaxing on the beach is the place to be.

Autumn
- **A** utumn time, bonfires blazing
- **U** p above fireworks, amazing
- **T** rees turn orange, yellow and brown
- **U** ntil the leaves come tumbling down.

M onsters roaming in the streets
N ight is full of tricks and treats.

Winter
W inter is cold, long, dark nights
I cicles and fairy lights
N ativity scene, Jesus born in a stable
T urkey and stuffing laid on the table
E xcitement is high
R eindeer in the sky.

Matthew Rutherford (9)
Rickleton Primary School, Washington

My Nanna's Ears

My nanna's ears don't work very well,
She doesn't hear the things we tell.
So I might say, 'How are you today?'
She thinks I've said, 'I'm going out to play.'

'We are just popping into town.'
Sounds like, 'Your trousers are falling down.'
'Is the weather warm and dry?'
'Yes, for dinner I had some pie.'

'Bye Nanna, I'm off to school!'
'Did you say you'd seen a ghoul?'
'I'll see you soon, at 3:30.'
'What? Justin Bieber's coming round for tea?'

'Hey Nanna, I've seen the bin man!'
'Where is a gorilla with a frying pan?'
I don't want Nanna to get a hearing aid,
Because that's how all the fun is made!

Tess Guthrie (9)
Rickleton Primary School, Washington

The Football Match

Football is exciting,
But it's not to everybody's liking.
The manager is doubting,
The fans are shouting.
The other team hits the back of the net,
Yet again, we are going to lose our bet.
At half-time,
The manager starts to whine.
The fans start to give up,
We're never going to win the cup.
A new striker is brought to the team,
And the smiles on the players start to beam.
The second half gets underway,
This might finally be the day.
The crowd does a Mexican wave,
As the goalkeeper does an amazing save.
A hat-trick is scored by the super striker sub,
The fans go celebrating to the pub.

Oliver Hay (9)
Rickleton Primary School, Washington

Dreams

Before I sail off in my bed
I snuggle up with my ted.
Then I zoom off up into space
Landing on a soft bed of lace.
I find myself dancing across the stage
Dreaming my dream, page by page.
Around me are soft, purple clouds
And peaceful music all around.
There are good sides and bad sides,
Nightmares and dreams,
Sometimes everything is not all that it seems.
There are rainbows and unicorns
And ghosts and ghouls,
Spectacular castles, surrounded by pools.
There are mountains and rivers
And cities and towns,
Princesses in palaces with beautiful gowns.
There are towers of doom
And flowers that bloom.
Will I awake very soon?

And then, my eyes open to the start of the day,
Waiting for my dreams to take me away.

Sasha Kate Latimer (10)
Rickleton Primary School, Washington

The Unnamed Thief

He came in the night
and took many things.
His big black bag, swinging
by his side.

He stole my pearl earrings,
even the baby, who cried.
I sat up in bed, watching
the black silhouette.
I couldn't stay awake
no matter how I tried.

He took the big blue clock
tick, tick, tock.
Oh!
He broke my lock.
Why? Why? Why?
Did he even try?
He pinched the lamp
although it was damp.

When I woke that morning,
the wallpapered walls were bare, so I knew,
he'd left, he'd left,
he'd left.
Nothing was left.

He was the unnamed thief.

Jenna Everett (10)
Rickleton Primary School, Washington

Ghoul School

I went to school,
With a ghoul,
Where the lightning crackled down.
I went to school,
With a ghoul,
Whose face was always a frown.
I went to school,
With a ghoul,
Whose name was Peter Jack.
I went to school,
With a ghoul,
Who had a big, black sack.
I went to school,
With a ghoul,
Whose mum's name was Grace.
I went to school,
With a ghoul,
Who had a hairy face.
I went to school,
With a ghoul,
Whose sister was called Mary.

I went to school,
With a ghoul,
Who dressed up like a fairy.
I went to school,
With a ghoul
And to be honest, he wasn't that scary.

Amy Bell (10)
Rickleton Primary School, Washington

Autumn Is Coming

Rustle.
Rustle.
The trees swaying.
The leaves start to fall down
Turning red, gold and brown.
When the cold north wind blows
It freezes me, from my toes to my nose.
Through the crispy, crunchy leaves I run,
I'm laughing because I'm having lots of fun.
I love walking down the streets at Halloween,
Looking at all the ghosts that make me scream!
With my family, I walk terrifying, creepy streets,
Knocking on doors, collecting bags of sweets.
On the bonfire, Guy Fawkes hangs.
Ear-splitting bangs,
Fireworks dazzling bright,
I love Bonfire Night.
Autumn.

Matthew Jones (9)
Rickleton Primary School, Washington

The Night-Time Knocker

I went to bed at 10 o'clock and what
did I hear in the night-time?
Knock, knock, knock, knock.

So I went downstairs to open the door
and what did I see? Nothing. Hmm.

Then I went back upstairs to bed and what
did I hear in the night-time? *Knock.*
So I got my mum and dad to open the door
and what did we see? Nothing.

I woke up the next day and what did I hear?
Silence
so I went outside to see who was there and there
was nobody.

Then I saw a man in my garden and he was the
night-time knocker, knocker, knocker, knocker!

Rajan Singh (9)
Rickleton Primary School, Washington

The Pokémon Rap

Pikachu!
I choose you!
Froakie!
Fights as well too!

Pidgey show them
what you've got!
Charmander
Use flame shot!

Ash Ketchum is a boy
from Pallet Town!
He wants to bring
the other trainers to the ground!

He wants to get
all the Pokémon!
That's the main event
in this song!

He meets a couple
of friends on his way!

Brock, Misty,
Clementine and May!

His friends stay with him
throughout his journey!
Want to learn some more?
Watch the programme and see!

Jack Andrew Lawson (9)
Rickleton Primary School, Washington

Autumn Is Here!

Summer has ended and autumn is here,
it's my favourite time of the year!
Kicking leaves, collecting conkers,
colours of copper and gold.
Days get colder, wrap up warm;
nights get longer, stay indoors.
Hot chocolate and blankets, nights by the fire,
sweets, treats and frights on Halloween night!
Bang! go the fireworks, *crackle!* goes the fire,
Bonfire Night is awesome as rockets fly higher.
My birthday comes next, with presents and cake,
I wonder if I'll get anything to make?
Autumn is cool, I like it a lot,
but winter is coming and that is not!

Aimee Mae Harrison (10)
Rickleton Primary School, Washington

Football

I really love football,
even though I'm not that tall.
Some matches are away,
so I practise every day.
One day I tackled a player too hard,
so I got the warning of a yellow card.
Playing football is a dream,
I will still play when I'm sixteen.
My parents are very proud
even when I am very loud.
I work hard at training,
even if it's raining.
I want to become a star,
but I'll never get that far.
I have more pace
when I tie my lace.
Football moments are what I will treasure,
as I look on to my new adventure!

Nathan Rajeev (10)
Rickleton Primary School, Washington

Family

It's sometimes hard to put into words just what I'd like to say,
But always know, you're thought of in a very special way.
Though the distance between us keeps us miles apart,
There'll always be a special place for you within my heart.
My brother is a dragon,
My mom is a teddy bear.
I am a shaggy sheepdog with a ton of tangled hair.
My father is a monkey, he likes to make us laugh,
Especially my sister, who is a tall giraffe.
We are a busy family with many things to do,
Our home is always happy, but sometimes it's a zoo.

Damarah Middlemas (9)
Rickleton Primary School, Washington

Minecraft Rap

Yo, this is the Minecraft rap.
If you don't play Minecraft, you're gonna get a *slap!*

If you're the murderer, you get a knife
and if you're being chased by the murderer,
you'll be running for your life.

The animal that you don't see is ducks
and if you die, well, that sucks.

Hypixel is the place for you,
a new map in bed, that's new.

Well this is the end of Minecraft rap
and if you still don't play Minecraft,
you're gonna get a bigger *slap!*

Lincoln Adamson (9)
Rickleton Primary School, Washington

Autumn

Conkers and acorns fall down from the trees,
The leaves on the ground are crisp and crunchy.
The leaves are red, orange, yellow and brown
And all are so bright, colourful and bold.

Everyone goes blackberry picking,
To make delicious pies and crumble.
Baked in the oven to stop tummies' rumble,
As the leaves outside start to tumble.

Children are playing in the park,
As leaves crunch under their feet.
Sycamore seeds get thrown in the air,
Oh, what a treat!

Grab your coat, let's go!

Ella McNally (9)
Rickleton Primary School, Washington

Autumn's Here

A utumn leaves lie on the ground
U nder the trees you hear a sound,
T wigs, *snap, crackle, pop.*
U mbrellas are sheltering us from the rain
M isty mornings are coming around
N ow winter is on its way, so get ready for Santa Claus. Hooray!
S now will soon fall from the sky.

H ere are the colourful leaves
E verybody gets excited because autumn is here
R ain will fall and sometimes the sun will shine
E very day gets colder because autumn is here.

Ellie Grace Bramley (9)
Rickleton Primary School, Washington

Animals

When I ride a horse, it makes me feel free.
The types of animals, one represents me!
I sit with my rabbit whilst having my tea,
Which makes me happy as can be.

My rabbit is fluffy, fluffy as can be.
If you came to my house you would clearly see.
She hops and she jumps and looks at me,
Whilst I am giving her her tea.

When I look in a mirror, what do I see?
A girl who loves horses looking back at me.

Animals are my life and I love them so much
And one day soon, I will have a lot.

Lily-May Gould (9)
Rickleton Primary School, Washington

Freedom

Trapped, alone
Within a gloomy cage.
'Oh please, someone! Help me get out.'
If only I could be free.

When I become free,
I will explore my mysterious world;
Soaring, forever, round and round,
To observe all the animals, country to country.

I would love to meet my family one time,
I will find my family
However long it takes me.
Who knows, I could have really rich parents.

Not all birds are granted freedom,
But I'm a blue budgie and now
I'm *free!*

Amelia Ava Goodwin (9)
Rickleton Primary School, Washington

My Dog

My dog, Rex, sits by the door,
His nose pointed hopefully at his lead.
'All right boy,' I say and I pull on my shoes.
Rex runs in circles, all tangled in his lead,
Nudging my pocket for treats.
'Let's go Rex,' I say.
A bike is the only way to keep up with my collie's speed.
Finally, off his lead, he greets other dogs with loud barks.
Back home, he searches for his blue bowl,
His big tongue flicks water across the floor,
Settled in his basket, he slowly falls asleep.

Adam Davies (9)
Rickleton Primary School, Washington

The Yoda Rap

His name is Yoda,
He is short and green
And he is a lean, mean fighting machine.
He can't be beaten,
He's got the Force,
He's got the Jedi Council.
If you want to beat him,
Ask him for advice,
Dagobah is his planet,
He lives there in good peace.
If you go there, like Luke Skywalker,
Don't get tricked by his appearance,
Because he will hurt you lots.
Don't try to beat him with the Force,
He will tie you into knots.
That's the Yoda Rap!

Louis Cutler (9)
Rickleton Primary School, Washington

All I Want

All I want is friendship
is that too much to ask?
All I want is friendship
to forget the things in my past.
All I want is friendship
to take away the tears and pain.
All I want is friendship
to never feel that way again.

All I have is friendship
to make me laugh and smile.
All I have is friendship
to make it worthwhile.
All I have is friendship
to hold on to my memories.
All I have is friendship
now I don't have any enemies.

Keerat Singh Uppal (9)
Rickleton Primary School, Washington

When I Play Football

When I play football,
I'm part of the team.
We pull together
to score the winning goals.

When I play football,
I am very active.
My heart races like a sports car
going at full speed.

When I play football,
I'm often in goal.
I jump around like a kangaroo,
trying to save all the shots.

When I play football,
I get 'man of the match'.
I get all of the glory
and a pat on the back.

Adam Kean (9)
Rickleton Primary School, Washington

Cats Wear Hats

Big cats, little cats wear hats
Black cats, white cats, grey cats and tabby cats.
Fluffy cats, smooth cats, tatty cats can wear hats.
Kittens in the kitchen, leopards in the laundry,
Snow leopards up in the mountain,
Lions in the jungle can wear hats.
Tigers in the zoo, wildcat up a tree,
They all like hats.

Red hats, black hats, white hats,
Woolly hats, soft hats, paper hats too.

Hats, hats, hats,
Choose a purr-fect hat.

Lydia Laidler (10)
Rickleton Primary School, Washington

The Best Memories

Making dens in the trees
And getting stung by nettles and bees
Are the best things
I love about the caravan.

Swimming in the sparkling, cold river
And try not to shake and shiver
Are all the best things
I love about the caravan.

Swinging from long, frayed ropes
And riding lakes on motorboats
Are all the best things
I love about the caravan.

When I grow up, my kids
Will definitely have a caravan.

Daniel Robson (10)
Rickleton Primary School, Washington

Minecraft

Minecraft, Minecraft, what would you do?
I like to throw slime balls made out of goo.
Perhaps you could craft a humorous house,
Or if you wish you could get a mouse.
Make a bed fast
Or you'll be in a blast!
Mine some gold,
It will make you bold!
You could be a builder,
If you mine some silver.
You could have a cat
That looks like a bat.
Minecraft, Minecraft, whatever you do
I hope you have had some great clues!

Emily Pauc (9)
Rickleton Primary School, Washington

Minecraft Survival

Starting a game,
I'm choosing a place.
Crafting my tools,
to build my base.

I'm cutting lots of wood,
I'm killing some sheep.
Got to make a bed,
so I can sleep.

Got to do some mining,
for iron, gold and stones,
I'll kill some skeletons
to give me bones.

I want to tame a wolf,
I want to grow some crops,
This game can last forever,
I hope it never stops.

Cadon Howarth (10)
Rickleton Primary School, Washington

Fright In The Night - A Rhyme

There was a knock on Halloween night,
I got out of bed, it gave me a fright.
I crept down the hallway silent as a mouse,
I sneaked to the door of my fairly small house.
I opened the door and poked my head out
But there was no stirring in or about.
I turned round to face a horrible creature
Its razor-sharp teeth, a terrifying feature.
It lunged towards me and opened its mouth
But as soon as I squealed, it darted off south.

Mark Patterson (10)
Rickleton Primary School, Washington

Mythical Mash-Up

Zeus, Poseidon, Hades
And a few more ladies,
Work together,
Now and forever.

Cyclops, Titan and more,
Make the mortals soar.
Monsters here, monsters there,
Monsters everywhere.

Roman, Greek and Norse,
Myths galore.
Enemies or friends
At other ends.

Zeus, Poseidon, Hades
And a few more ladies,
Work together,
Now and forever.
That's the mythical mash-up!

Elliot Jordan Curry (10)
Rickleton Primary School, Washington

Family

My name is Imi,
you're going to open your ears and listen.
My sister is Olivia,
she pulls funny faces and she is very graceful.
My mum is Joanne,
her favourite breakfast is jam and crumpets.
My dad is gentle, he's kind,
he takes me out and places we can always find.
My grandma is generous
and she will always look after me.
Grandad is grumpy when he is tired,
but he loves me and my little sister!

Imogen Lucy Moat (9)
Rickleton Primary School, Washington

Autumn

When autumn rolls around,
at 5 o'clock it's dark.
The leaves fall off trees,
the animals hibernate, the hedgehogs and the bees.
People wear hats, gloves and scarves,
to keep themselves warm in the dark.
Halloween rolls around,
you can see people carving pumpkins
and little kids dressed as Munchkins.
When Bonfire Night is here,
in the dark,
you can see the sparks
of the bonfires.

Evie Grace Shield (10)
Rickleton Primary School, Washington

Halloween Night

Halloween comes once a year
go trick-or-treating
if you dare.

This is the time of year
where ghosts come out the most

Monsters and witches
hiding in ditches.

There's hands popping out of graves,
you'd better be brave.

Kids dress up and go trick or treating,
be careful you might get eaten.

Are you brave enough?

Grace Winter (11)
Rickleton Primary School, Washington

My Big Sister

Even though she fights
and gets mad
she will always be
my big sister.

She is tall and helpful
when I fall she will
pick me right up
again.

Her name is Jessica
and she will always
be my big sister.

Something can go wrong
and she will get sad and nervous
but she knows I will be there and I know
she will be there for me.

Jasmine Dhillon (9)
Rickleton Primary School, Washington

December Days

D ecember days are nice and long, fun for everyone.
E very day hold a new surprise.
C ome inside and have some mince pies.
E ach day brings a promise of snow.
M y sledge is ready, ready to go.
B alls of snow ready to fire.
E veryone duck, my aim is higher.
R emember, it's my birthday too! And Santa's coming to visit you!

James Michael Southern (9)
Rickleton Primary School, Washington

My Love Of Life

I love my friends and
I love my family,
I love to spend time
with everybody.

I love to walk and
I love to run,
I love to do everything
that is fun.

My world is full of
everything I love,
from the Earth below
to the heavens above.

I say a word and
I say a prayer and
I ask for all
please to care.

Brooke Northey (9)
Rickleton Primary School, Washington

My Brother

My brother got out the pool and
drip, drip, dripped...
My brother emptied the bin and
it bash, bash, bashed...
My brother burst my balloon and
it pop, pop, popped...
My brother dropped the cup and
it smash, smash, smashed...
My brother hit the floor and
it crack, crack, cracked...
And that's who the
clumsy man was.

Cuan Snell (10)
Rickleton Primary School, Washington

Football

My favourite game is football
I play it every day
Sometimes I kick it against the wall
I think I do okay.

I play for some different teams
But the goal is always the same
We want to fulfil our dreams
And earn ourselves the fame.

Sometimes we lose
Sometimes we win
We don't get to choose
But it helps us keep thin.

Jake Lish (9)
Rickleton Primary School, Washington

Pleasure Craft

Turning on my Xbox
I start to feel the pleasure
from creating new landscapes
and new buildings to measure.
Select materials and tools
start to lay foundations.
Soon I see the results
of my latest creations.

Hours and hours of happiness
from all things new.
Are there better pastimes?
There can only be a few!

Arin Cohan (9)
Rickleton Primary School, Washington

Me And My Sisters

Sisters are forever, forever in the world,
My sisters are my best friends, I tell the whole world.

We share our clothes, we share the joy
And the sorrows.

We fight with each other for no good reason,
We stand up for each other.

We annoy each other, can't stop,
We are always together, no matter what.

Amrit Kaur Dulai (10)
Rickleton Primary School, Washington

Forest

Leaves lie in the breeze, then stop
and drop on the ground with leaves.
The trees dance in the distance.

Flowers smile at me,
fern's patterns attract me to stare at them.

The sun beams at me
ready for the morning.

The snuffly hedgehog retreats,
no more owls echoing in the trees.

Casey James Ritchie (10)
Rickleton Primary School, Washington

My Weekend In Blackpool

It was very wet, the sun was set,
and thousands of lights shone so bright.
The Tower lit up in the night
and was a beautiful sight.
We walked all the way along the shore,
until our feet and toes were really sore.
We caught the tram back,
which rode along the track.
We all thought it was great
and stayed up very late.

Edie Rebecca Macbeth (9)
Rickleton Primary School, Washington

Embers

Bright vibrant sparks
Dancing through the night,
Sprinkling all around,
Lighting up the sky.
Smouldering, blazing flames,
Heating up my face,
I feel innocuous
And most safe.
But the rain comes down,
Drip by drip,
Quenching the ground,
Putting paid to the glittering flames,
Replaced by embers fading away.

Dixie Martha Baker (10)
Rickleton Primary School, Washington

My Family

Mum and Dad as sweet as can be,
Brother's a typical teen,
Sister, make-up, wants to be a tattoo artist,
The big, beady eyes are the cutest
Of my adorable two dogs.
Brother is annoying
And sister is too,
But the best thing I could hear from them is,
'I love you!'
I love my family
And they love me too!

Kayleigh Rafferty (10)
Rickleton Primary School, Washington

Sun And Moon

Bright lights,
cool breeze.
Sun so bright,
it's blinding me.

Blue skies,
soft winds.
The moon is so beautiful,
as it fills my eyes with glee.

But when the shadowy eclipse arrives,
we are a pitch-black world
and as the moon carefully moves,
we are no longer in a darkened world.

Emily Bradney (9)
Rickleton Primary School, Washington

Holiday Times

H ow great are holidays?
O ut and about having fun.
L ots of happy family memories are made.
I n different countries, you can try new things.
D ifferent places, different cultures.
A ny country, you can visit and explore.
Y our next destination awaits, adventures, smells and new tastes.

Anna Jayne Whitfield (9)
Rickleton Primary School, Washington

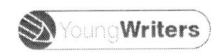

The Dream Catcher

Don't go to sleep, don't go to sleep, something is in the air,
the Dream Catcher's there.
If you go to sleep, if you close your eyes,
he will steal your dreams, but no one knows why.
If the Dream Catcher gets you,
don't let it come as a surprise.
I have warned you very clear,
the Dream Catcher is here.

Elisha Turnbull (11)
Rickleton Primary School, Washington

Bedtime

It's 8:30 and all is great.
Watching Smurfs because they are great.

The clock strikes nine and all is fine,
but I hate that time.

It's time for bed,
a time I dread.

It's time for sleep,
my little Bo Peep.

Just remember
to brush your teeth.

Logan Green (10)
Rickleton Primary School, Washington

People

People aren't always friendly.
People aren't always happy.
People never always smile.
People never always frown.
Some people may be sad.
Some people may be unhappy.
Some people choose to be upset.
Some people choose to stay single,
Which is why they never mingle!

Rebecca Marsh (10)
Rickleton Primary School, Washington

Wind

How I love my pumps to stink
It really makes you stop and think
What was it I had
That makes them smell so bad?

They make everyone leave the room
Light a match, it would go *boom!*
I cock my leg and see their dread
Up they jump and escape to the shed.

Nathan Alcock (9)
Rickleton Primary School, Washington

Thanos

T itan, menacing mad.
H is Infinity gauntlet glimmering in the light.
A s the ship door closes
N earer, closer... He's coming!
O ver light years, his quest continues.
S trongly, the Avengers pull themselves from the crater - they are ready

Max Burlison (10)
Rickleton Primary School, Washington

Minecraft Life

Minecraft in the morning,
Minecraft in the evening,
Finding the jewels,
To make the best tools.

Dig a hole to hide,
Get a saddle to ride.
Make a friend to play,
Build a house to stay.
Searching, digging, killing,
It's all so thrilling.

Priya Seren Dhindsa (9)
Rickleton Primary School, Washington

Winter Snow

Winter snow is very cold
In the winter, Christmas will come.

All the presents you will get
You want money
You want sweets
I want snow
So do you.
Deep down, you know you do
Snow, snow, come, come,

We love snow.

Sophie Dunn (9)
Rickleton Primary School, Washington

Autumn Has Arrived

Chilly morning air,
Crispy leaves crunching under my feet.
I walked through a pumpkin patch
They're waiting to be picked.

Spices in the air
Pumpkins everywhere...
Halloween is approaching,
Autumn has arrived.

Callum Morrison (11)
Rickleton Primary School, Washington

Cosy!

The nights draw in cold and dark
Candles on and curtains drawn
Woolly hats and thick socks
The wind picks up
The leaves fall down
Beef stew and shepherd's pie
Pie and peas
It's cosy, it's cosy, it's cosy!

Grace Elizabeth Hewitt (11)
Rickleton Primary School, Washington

What Makes Me Happy

What makes me happy is the sky turning blue,
Being happy, being happy, you should try it too.
Being happy can last for a while,
Being happy is the Harriet style.
Music, TV, you should try it soon.
Being happy is fun to do.

Harriet Georgia Dunn (9)
Rickleton Primary School, Washington

My Unicorn's Style

I have a pet unicorn
With a pointy horn.
She wears a dressing gown
with a frown to town.
She goes to the mall
wearing a shawl.
She cleans in jeans.
That's my unicorn's style.

Amelia Isabelle Lowden (10)
Rickleton Primary School, Washington

The Hottest Day Of The Year

On the hottest day of the year,
we play at the beach.
On the hottest day of the year,
we play hide-and-go-seek.
On the hottest day of the year,
we rest and have fun, all in the sun.

Jon-James Robert Ware (10)
Rickleton Primary School, Washington

Frogs

F rogs are my favourite animals.
R ibbit is what they do.
O f course they're small.
G ood for them too
S o off they go, jumping about!

Charlie William Miller (11)
Rickleton Primary School, Washington

Mountains And Valleys

Mountains are high,
Valleys are low.
Eagles waiting for prey to die below.
Scramblers scrambling up the sides,
Campers camping in the valley below.

Ben Hovvels (9)
Rickleton Primary School, Washington

Minecraftpedia

Fire grows
Lava glows, ice melts
Water freezes
Grass grows, wheat dies,
Lights fade
Darkness falls
Don't sleep
Mine it all.

Zachary Wheat (10)
Rickleton Primary School, Washington

Sun And Moon

(A diamante poem)

Sun
Bright, blazing
fire, orange, burning.
Dawn, life, dusk, night
silver, stillness, peace.
Rocket, explore
Moon.

Innes Batey (10)
Rickleton Primary School, Washington

Football

Football makes me feel happy
Football is my dream
Whenever I score a goal
I feel fantastic
And I always have great fun!

Nathan Olley (10)
Rickleton Primary School, Washington

Time

Waiting, waiting, waiting for this very time,
when will it come?

Waiting, waiting, waiting for this very time,
almost there, come on clock have some fun.

Waiting, waiting, waiting for this very time,
yes, time to run.

Run, run, run to the finish line,
I can see this race being mine.

Whoops! I don't believe it, another racer is catching me up,
I need to find some extra speed to win that cup.

I'm in the lead, the finishing line is in my sight,
I've won the race, yes!

Caleb Shay Buckingham (8)
St Oswald's RC Primary School, South Shields

Shark Attack

The great white shark loves to bite,
Don't get too close or he'll give you a fright.
He is very, very fast,
If you're in a race, you're bound to be last.

When you're in the sea, he'll gobble you up,
He's not as cute as a newborn pup.
Sharks are mostly found in hot countries,
He'll gobble you up like a pack of Munchies.

Sharks can come up to catch their prey,
They also hunt both night and day.
The largest shark is a great white,
It also has the largest bite.

Under the sea, sharks can hide in shipwrecks,
It hurts way more than when a bird pecks.
They have pointy fins and breathe with gills,
Sharks swim and glide, gills are on the shark's side.

The biggest shark used to be the megalodon, but it is now extinct,
So you can't feel being jabbed with flint.

People can see them down in a cage,
Be a good swimmer, depends on your age.

Go down the slide, landing in the sea,
If you see a shark, he'll invite you for tea.

Bite, bite, bite,
Fight, fight, fight,
Bite, bite, bite,
Fight, fight, fight.

Be careful in the sea!

Harry James Wales (8)
St Oswald's RC Primary School, South Shields

Recipe For Chocolate Cake

For cake I've got the right cure,
I'm pretty sure.
Making cake is so easy,
Especially if it's chocolate cake.

Get the baking tray,
In the middle of May,
Don't forget your bowl!
Add the whitest flour,
Crack the eggs into the mixer,
The egg yolk
Is no joke!
Add the sweet sugar,
Mix it up
And put it in the oven to bake,
To make your chocolate cake.

When you take it out of the oven,
Squirt, squirt on the chocolate cream,
Don't dream!

Add some rainbow sprinkles,
Into the oven goes the cake,
For another little bake.

This time put a bit of melted chocolate in the middle,
Squash in a chocolate wafer and Flake,
Plop on some whipped cream
And finally, slide on some ice cream.
Presto! You've completed your cake.
Now a quick taste test and...
Yum-yum, it's delicious.
Now try and make it for yourself

Joe Steel (9)
St Oswald's RC Primary School, South Shields

What Is Peace?

Peace is eternal love,
As quiet as night,
As gentle as a dove,
As white as a dove,
But not even peace is perfect!

Always loving and caring,
As loving as God,
Alone time and happy places,
Being a peacemaker, like Jesus.

As peaceful as peace,
As loving as God,
As relaxing as sleep,
Never too hard to be a peacemaker.

Marissa Towns (8)
St Oswald's RC Primary School, South Shields

I Am A Parrot

I am a parrot,
I live in a cage,
I walk and talk,
I even say my owner's name.

I used to live in a forest,
I used to be free.
I flew around like crazy
And I sang with glee.

But then, I got caught
And now I live in a zoo,
No more fun for me,
Please let me be free.
Please,
Please,
Please.

Poppy Grace Melia (9)
St Oswald's RC Primary School, South Shields

My Name Is... - An Acrostic Poem

R uby is my name.
U nder the sea is my favourite place.
B acon is my favourite food.
Y ap, yap is all I do.

L una means moon in Spanish.
U nicorns are so cool.
N ail painting is so much fun.
A rt is my favourite thing to do.

Ruby Calvert (8)
St Oswald's RC Primary School, South Shields

My Pet Parrot

I'm a cheeky pet parrot
and my favourite food is carrot
in my cage, I love to walk
and I like to squawk.
Squawk, squawk
I am loud
and make a lot of sound.
I make fun of people's voices
the owners of me love me with joy.

Toby Male (8)
St Oswald's RC Primary School, South Shields

What Am I?

Nest maker
High flyer
Loud squawker
Worm lover
Cat chaser.

Orange beak
People friendly
Cheerful tweeter
Food eater.

What am I?

Rebecca Louise Robson (8)
St Oswald's RC Primary School, South Shields

Kennings Poem

High flyer
Loud squawker
Brilliant singer
Nest builder
Cheeky talker
Worm eater
Copy worder
Shoulder lover.

What am I?

Stevey Louise Burrough (8)
St Oswald's RC Primary School, South Shields

What Am I?

Cat hater,
nest maker
worm eater,
fish eater.

Egg layer,
little legs,
multicoloured,
mice eater,
what am I?

Rebecca Stonehouse (8)
St Oswald's RC Primary School, South Shields

Ducks

Water liker
head bobber
happy pecker
big tail.

Loud quacker
leaf looker
egg layer
fast swimmer.

Oliver Stirling Welsh (8)
St Oswald's RC Primary School, South Shields

What Am I?
(A kennings poem)

Loud barker
Fluffy and mucky
Rough player
Fast eater
Springy jumper
Cute runner
Bone lover
Love sleeper.

Noah Robinson (8)
St Oswald's RC Primary School, South Shields

Freedom

Freedom is playing, fun and friends.
Freedom is school, sleep and exploring.
Freedom is education, love who you want and fairness.
Freedom is playing on the PS4, food and bike riding.
Freedom is playing games, watching Mother and experiments.
Freedom is golf, playing on consoles and holidays.

Harley Celino (9)
Trinity Academy - Deneview, South Gosforth

Untitled

Water evaporates into the sky,
and to clouds
and forms down the mountainside,
it soaks into the ground
to hide and comes up
to crash and thrash
and thrive and bend like elastic,
getting wider and thinner
until it starts piling
up over the rocks and getting
faster and stronger
gaining momentum
going to the sea,
the place it wants to be,
with the soil deposits cutting it off
but it's still on its way,
curving around
everything in its way
or piling on top of it,

until it gets to the sea
and everything calms down
into a big body of water
where the river ends.

Bradley Walters (10)
Trinity Academy - Deneview, South Gosforth

The River's Journey

A river is a warm shadow
that gently flows through the muddy, green water.
With trees growing alongside the river,
the moss covering the rocks
as they stand still in the flowing river
waiting for something to happen.
The river makes roads for boats
and helps feed people with food and water.

Llayton Wharton (10)
Trinity Academy - Deneview, South Gosforth

Freedom

Freedom is you can do what you want.
Freedom is playing what you want.
Freedom is loving who you want.
Freedom is not being locked out.
Freedom is wearing what you want.
Freedom is having a choice.
Freedom is treating people fairly.

Joshua Hunter (9)
Trinity Academy - Deneview, South Gosforth

Freedom

I'm a scary dog, a running dog,
Jumping through the lava dog.
I'm a YouTuber dog, a playing dog,
A space dog and a good dog.
I am a cute dog, a free dog,
And never in my cage dog.

Alfie Watts (7)
Trinity Academy - Deneview, South Gosforth

Freedom

Freedom is playing out on your bike.
Freedom is playing on your PlayStation.
Freedom is playing football with my dad.
Freedom is playing with the dog.
Freedom is going on a steam train.

Nathan Johnston (9)
Trinity Academy - Deneview, South Gosforth

Freedom

Freedom is playing out on my bike.
Freedom is going to the park.
Freedom is playing football with friends.
Freedom is fishing.
Freedom is playing with ferrets.

Leighton Turnbull (9)
Trinity Academy - Deneview, South Gosforth

Freedom

I'm a big dog, a white dog
A playing with a bone dog.
I'm a happy dog
I'm a brown dog
A running through the water dog.

Kai Forrest (7)
Trinity Academy - Deneview, South Gosforth

Rotten Rhymes

A dog mess,
Rotten cress.
Yucky bugs,
Lizard lugs.
Furry, fat rat,
Ugly, bitter cat.
Scary ship,
Metal tip.

Elisha Collinson (9)
Trinity Academy - Deneview, South Gosforth

Freedom

I'm big dog, a happy dog
A playing, chewing, running dog.
I'm a brown dog, a white dog
A walking, jumping, saving dog.

Shane Mills (7)
Trinity Academy - Deneview, South Gosforth

Freedom

I'm a nice dog, a fast dog
A running in a field dog.
I'm a funny dog,
A sporty dog
A jumping on a log dog.

Robert Hurst (8)
Trinity Academy - Deneview, South Gosforth

Freedom

I am a glad dog, a good dog
A mad, bad and sad dog.
I am a Netflix dog, a jumping dog
A free dog and a running dog.

Charlie Scott (7)
Trinity Academy - Deneview, South Gosforth

Rotten Rhymes

Rotten vegetables,
Squid tentacles.
Smelly socks,
Scary black box.
Lions' tails,
Slimy snails.

Caine Campbell (9)
Trinity Academy - Deneview, South Gosforth

Freedom

I am a mad dog, fast dog
Funny, jumping, happy dog.
I'm a scary dog, a jumpy dog
A running on the mud dog.

Louis Maughan (8)
Trinity Academy - Deneview, South Gosforth

Building My Biome

Just to begin, make a new world.
Call it your biome
And add on a new word.
Press on, create,
Build a few trees.
A village if you want,
Then build your house.
Six blocks wide as well as tall
Add some windows along with the door,
Then do some mining.
Find some coal and *woah*, look!
Gold, iron and diamonds galore
Go make a sword, pickaxe and axe,
Then make your shovel.
Leave the hoe for last.
Get some obsidian,
Enough for another portal,
Kill some pig men,
Then finish your home.
Oh my, oh my, an Ender portal.
Must get ready to finish the game,

I've crafted the armour,
Enchanted the bow,
I think I've done everything,
Now let's go.
Oh no, oh no, I forgot my wolf,
Now all I have is hope.
Destroyed all the healing stations,
Now Ender Dragon's low on health.
Must kill him now,
Or I'll die as well.
Yes, yes I've done it,
I won.
Now finally, I must collect all the EXP,
I've completed my biome,
But now I must think,
Will I have time to do it again?

Robert William McGuffog (9)
Wellfield Middle School, Whitley Bay

Swim, Dance, Repeat

S tanding on the block, wanting the race to start.
W hen the whistle blows, a perfect race begins.
I nto the lead I go, my legs are kicking fast.
M y fingers touch first and a golden medal is my reward.

D reading my exam, I wait nervously outside the room.
A fter all the practising, the moment of truth has come.
N ow I am dancing and spinning, I feel my confidence return.
C almly stepping out the room, knowing I have done well.
E ventually, after all the patient waiting, my results coming.

R emember practice makes perfect if you try.
E very week I practise till my arms are aching.
P lenty of times, I felt like I was too tired to go.
E xcellent competitions, my friends keep me company.

A ll the hard work and training, it will pay off in the end.
T o be a good sport player, you should never give up.

Katie Coventry (10)
Wellfield Middle School, Whitley Bay

My Best Friend

I wake up today looking for my socks
Trying to find this thief
The sound of munching echoes through the house.

Climbing into my onesie, I race down the stairs
Entering the kitchen,
I discover her here, destroying a mountain of kibble.

Guarding socks, not letting anyone cross
My feet replaced with blocks of ice.

Lolloping, bounding, exploring
Suddenly, a flash of blonde
Speeding around faster than Mo Farah.

Bouncing into the field, there goes a kangaroo
Hopping and plopping
Appearing and disappearing from view.

Resting, relaxing, recovering now
Oh look, here it comes to snuggle
Guess who it is?

The wonder hound

Olive!

Charlie Pirie (9)
Wellfield Middle School, Whitley Bay

Homework? Uh... No!

Homework, homework!
It's so bad.
It's like teachers
want me to be sad.

Geography, geography!
It's so boring.
I'd rather be at home,
in my bed, snoring.

Division, division!
It's worse than hell.
I'd rather play Scrabble,
sitting in a well.

Times tables!
It's like I'm cursed.
Out of all my homework
it's definitely the worst.

I've got no time
to play with Will.

They'd rather have me learning
about a Shakespeare called Bill!

I do enough studying
when I'm in school.
Evenings are there for
me to be cool.

Oliver Wood (10)
Wellfield Middle School, Whitley Bay

Upside Down!

What happened to the world? It's all upside down
I don't understand and it is making me frown.

Flowers towering above my head
And trees down by my feet instead.
Fish are swimming in the sky
Birds that can talk and pigs that can fly.

The cheetah is racing as slow as a snail
The tortoise is so fast, he leaves no trail.
It's so very sad what happened to my dad
He can't even lift a twig and it's making him mad.

What happened to the world? It's all upside down
I don't understand and it is making me frown.

Now I have woken from the night
And everything's normal, to my delight!

Emily Morton (9)
Wellfield Middle School, Whitley Bay

My Perfect Day Of Each Season

In the early, frosty mornings,
when the sun is always shining, even though it's not blinding,
the sleeping seeds have been warmed,
so the flowers are awakening.

The summer days are long and sunny,
playing out, telling jokes that are funny,
you can climb trees when you please,
but have to avoid the bees.

As the crispy, crunchy leaves
fall from the trees,
they get gathered in a heap,
by the woodland creatures ready for their hibernation sleep.

The magic of the moonlight, sparkling on the snow
excites the waking children,
it's a day for building snowmen,
wrap up, let's go!

Amelia McClurry (9)
Wellfield Middle School, Whitley Bay

Night Under The Stars

I lost track of time!
The sun is going down,
Shadows lengthen,
Under-prepared, frightened, confused.

Need to build a shelter,
They are coming, coming.
Coming to get me,
Trying to stop me.

Those purple eyes in the distance,
Sudden flash of light, he's right beside me.
Look away, look away,
I'm not important enough for Enderman.

Once I collect iron,
I will build a sword.
I would teach those nasty mobs a lesson...
Once I build a sword.

I see the sun,
Rising in the east.
Relief flows over me,
That horrible night is done.

Ewan Sumby (9)
Wellfield Middle School, Whitley Bay

Mission Complete!

Dazzled by the mad world of Minecraft,
Stuck like superglue, how about that?
Leaping and diving to judge the enemy.
Gripping on for dear life, my body is heavy.
Fighting the lava flames, flicking bright,
Mining the blocks as smooth as ice.
Up they go, standing tall,
Creepers and zombies rise and fall.
Final adventure, here I come,
Running as fast as a cheetah is so much fun.
Knocking down blocks that are in my way,
I get better at mining every day.
I'm at the end of my adventure and I'm a winner,
Destination reached, my mission
Complete!

Vaughn Rhodes (9)
Wellfield Middle School, Whitley Bay

Ender Dragon

E nter the mine at your own risk.
N early there, the portal is close.
D are to take another step.
E yes of the Ender at the ready.
R esign yourself for the evil that stalks you out in the Ender.

D on't forget your pumpkin head.
R ight, jump into the portal.
A fter you shoot all the towers,
G et out all the weapons you have and get ready to stab the dragon with your diamond sword.
O nward you charge to wield your final blow.
N ow take the egg, your precious prize.

Niamh Caitlin Nicholson (9)
Wellfield Middle School, Whitley Bay

Can You Imagine?... Mmm

Can you imagine living in a world
where everything is made out of chocolate?

In winter, it's not snow, but chocolate so white,
Spring is so bright, it's such a delight.
Summers are hot, to melt white mice in queue,
But autumn is colourful with its caramel hues.

Milk chocolate rivers that shimmer with the light,
Mountains like Crunchies that crunch with a bite.
Grass as green as a Freddo frog
and clouds are fluffy, like marshmallow fog.

Mmmmm... yes, I *can* imagine a world of chocolate!

Eloise Conway (9)
Wellfield Middle School, Whitley Bay

Magic We Can't See

A devil's horn,
A demon's blood,
A unicorn's magic,
A wizard's wand,
A dragon's lair,
A skeleton's tomb,
A vampire's canine,
A time-travelling tree,
When you think carefully, it's true,
The magic might be looking back at you.

Lola Fischer (9)
Wellfield Middle School, Whitley Bay

Match Day

Sitting in the crowd where it was very loud,
the stadium of excited souls,
watched closely as they approached the goal.

At half-time, the score was 1-1
and we all cheered as they went back on.

Hoping that our team could score
to beat our rivals once more.

Finally, in added time
the ball managed to cross the line
to put us in front for the last time.

We walked out of the stadium with a smile on our face,
knowing that we finished in first place.

Louie Brown (9)
Wellfield Middle School, Whitley Bay

Football Is My Life

Saturday morning, up early
Meeting my friends at the pitch.
Dressed in my favourite football strip
Discussing tactic formations.
When we score, there will be celebrations.

Freezing weather, cold toes,
In my position, the whistle blows.
On a counter-attack, off I go,
Cross the ball, *bang*, what a goal!
They can't stop us, we are too fast,
Our team takes a shot and the ball slips past.
People on the sidelines cheering
Our names, but it is only a game.

Harrison Nisbet (9)
Wellfield Middle School, Whitley Bay

Create A World

Diamonds glittering bright in the night,
They're hidden, all out of sight.
They're very rare and hard to find,
But you have a clear picture in your mind.
Gather your tools and set to work,
Grab your pickaxe and go berserk.
Creepers and skeletons give you a fright
And zombies come out to fight.
All kinds of creatures roam the Nether,
This secret dimension goes on forever.
Create the world, build a town,
Mine out a swimming pool, knock a castle down.

Aaron Wood (9)
Wellfield Middle School, Whitley Bay

Baking Rocky Road

I love to bake rocky road,
It's better than eating a toad!
You don't have to go to Sainsbury's
To get a load of rocky road,
Just head down the dual carriageway
To Lucy France's house today!
Baking is lots of fun,
It's great for everyone!

Rocky road is delicious,
(However, it's not nutritious!)
But it is very precious.
I love to bake rocky road,
It's *so* much better than eating a toad!

Lucy France (9)
Wellfield Middle School, Whitley Bay

I Like Animals

A mazing dogs, never stop running along the beach.
N aughty cats, never stop catching mice and rats.
I ncredible hamsters, never stop spinning.
M ysterious mice, never stop disappearing out of sight.
A dorable puppies, never stop playing, sleeping and cuddling.
L ovely kittens, never stop scratching and climbing with their tiny paws.
S oft bunnies, never stop bouncing in the fields.

Matthew White (9)
Wellfield Middle School, Whitley Bay

Lightning!

Lethal strikes sent from the clouds,
Illuminating bolts from the raging storm,
Great handfuls of burning anger
Hacking at the earth, it slashes until it breaks.
Thrashing noises awake the great Earth in all its glory.
Nominated by the sphere above,
Lightning has been chosen to erupt from the sky.
It hurls rain with its side partner, together the world is fire.
Gigantic beams of light thrown from the almighty circle up high!

Oskar Armutcuoglu (9)
Wellfield Middle School, Whitley Bay

Space, Planets And Stars

Space is black, the stars are gold,
The sun shines bright against the starry sky; so bold.
The stars are fiery,
The sun is hot,
What makes it special, is the whole lot.
The moon reaches out when the sun goes down,
The solar system claps as the moon gleams all around.
The sun goes down, the moon comes up.
The Earth spins around giving life.
How grand and special is our universe?
Space is black, the stars are gold.

Maddy Coll (9)
Wellfield Middle School, Whitley Bay

My Dog's Life

Big brown eyes
and curly hair,
my dog Mango
is not allowed on the chair.

When Mum leaves the room,
I let her jump up.
I've been doing this
since she was a pup.

She doesn't like dog food,
how fussy is she?
So I feed her my food
when Mum cannot see.

I love my dog Mango,
she is the best,
but I don't love her enough
to pick up her mess.

Eoin Winder (9)
Wellfield Middle School, Whitley Bay

Herobrine

Herobrine comes in the dead of night
Chops down your house and sets it alight.
Steve, get your tools and get ready to fight
Don't let Herobrine see you in sight.
The time has come, I'm ready to fight
I've got my diamond armour, I've got my diamond sword.
Watch out Herobrine, I'm stronger than a Lord.
Herobrine is defeated, hooray, hooray!
I think I might have just completed the game.

Jake Humphrey (10)
Wellfield Middle School, Whitley Bay

A New World

Starting Minecraft this is what I see,
Many blocks right in front of me.
Grab wood, start to craft,
I'm on the road, on a brand-new path.
Got to stay clean, so I take a bath,
With my pickaxe mine some stone,
Wait! Is he made out of bone?
Then I looked down at my chest,
Saw an arrow come to rest.
I fell to the floor as my heart twirled,
But that's what happens in a brand-new world.

Alfie James Ord (10)
Wellfield Middle School, Whitley Bay

Newbies And Pros

Newbies and pros,
Swords and hoes,
Diamonds and dirt
Watch you don't hurt.

Scared of glass,
Scared of the end.
Hide from the creeper,
He's not your friend.

Build a mansion,
A hundred blocks wide,
Build a fortress,
The zombies died!

Build a dirt hut
And laugh at a pro,
If you're a noob,
Eat a poisonous potato.

Daniel Ross (10)
Wellfield Middle School, Whitley Bay

The Potion

The witches are gathered around the cauldron,
spellbook in hand, ingredients all prepared.
First some bat wings, frogs' legs, then dandelions,
adding a pinch of spiders' eyes.
Mixing altogether and chant the magic words,
the potion all mixed up,
it's time to test on the cat.
Pour it on and it shrinks to the size of a rat.
... Now to make the potion to turn her back!

Carley Coates (9)
Wellfield Middle School, Whitley Bay

My Love Of Gaming!

From Minecraft to Mario, I love them all,
Building houses big and small.
Completing level after level, Peach still gets lost,
Then I think I'd rather play Lara Croft.

Skylanders on my Xbox is my favourite by far,
I can even play my DS in the back of the car.

I get lost for hours in my gaming world of fun,
The adventures I have will never be done...

Daryl Davison (10)
Wellfield Middle School, Whitley Bay

Never Go There

Build a portal five blocks wide
Don't be scared, just watch your side.
Kill anything in sight, if you see an end and look away,
It's for your own good.
Kill, kill, quick as you can
Jump through the portal if you can.

Build a fort in the Nether
Go and kill the Ender Dragon.
Try not to mess up
Or you will be demolished in one swallow.

Tyler Ewart (9)
Wellfield Middle School, Whitley Bay

All Creatures Great And Small

What is that creature in that tree?
Up so high, making all the birds flee?

Is that a bug in the dirt?
Crawling around, if it bites it might hurt.

What's that bird in the air?
Swooping in the air, back to its secret lair.

All creatures great and small,
if you want to know what they are,
just give me a call.

Leo Richards (9)
Wellfield Middle School, Whitley Bay

Football 4 Life

F ootball is awesome.
O utstanding skill is required to play this game.
O ut in the rain, mud and grass.
T hrough rain, wind, sun and snow.
B ringing friends and competitors together.
A ll with one aim... To win.
L eaving the pitch with a sense of satisfaction.
L ove football. I love playing.

Charlie Payne (9)
Wellfield Middle School, Whitley Bay

Creeper Cave!

Mining in the cave,
when it's dark at night,
watch where you're stepping,
spiders are in sight.

Find a red block,
then you will see what's coming.
There it is,
a diamond is showing.

Creeper! Creeper!
Don't get in his way,
otherwise he'll do it,
he'll blow you away.

Emily Scott (9)
Wellfield Middle School, Whitley Bay

My Silly Dog Annie

Annie is as silly as my grandad, Billy.
She is always happy to see you when you walk through the door.
Even if it's only seconds, seconds you were gone for,
She is a teensy-weensy and extremely funny dog.
She is invisible in the fog, like a camouflage frog.
Lazy in the heat and her favourite food is animal meat!

Alfie Robert William Burnip (9)
Wellfield Middle School, Whitley Bay

The Egg

In the wastelands,
Everyone's a dead man.
Find the egg,
Find the egg.

The clashing of swords,
A flight to survival.
Get the egg,
Get the egg!

Blood,
Swords,
Slash,
Scream!

The dragon's egg
Is now gone.
This is not a bad dream!

Samuel Birkett (10)
Wellfield Middle School, Whitley Bay

Moby Mobs

Enderman, Enderman with purple eyes
Don't be scared by their disguise.
Jeepers creepers, short and green
Keep away from them they are awfully mean.
Ocelot, ocelot, don't be shy,
There is no reason to run and hide.
Bats, cats, there is a lot more than that,
Minecraft is where it is all at.

Morgan Smith (9)
Wellfield Middle School, Whitley Bay

Ice Cream

I like ice cream a whole lot
it tastes good when days are hot.

Strawberry, chocolate, vanilla too
with a Flake and sprinkles for you.

In a cone, or on a pie
it always catches my eye.

I love ice cream best of all,
it's been my favourite since I was small..

Eva Holly Pattison (9)
Wellfield Middle School, Whitley Bay

Minecraft Rocks

Creepers, creepers everywhere.
Don't go there or you'll be their prey.
If you hurt the dogs, they will hurt you.
Lava blocks, lava blocks
They'll hurt you.
Ice blocks, ice blocks
They'll freeze you.
Lead your dog so they don't hurt you.
So now you know what you can do

Harli-Mae Sydney Mawson (9)
Wellfield Middle School, Whitley Bay

Living In Ark

Surviving is a hard task
Bob awakens,
A blinding light smacks his eyes
In a land unknown.

On the inside of his wrist,
A milky, blue rhombus
Scorched, burnt in.

Raptors rustling rapidly
Dilophosaurus deadly, dangerous
Surviving is a hard task.

Dan Moll (9)
Wellfield Middle School, Whitley Bay

In The Water

S wimming, swimming all of my life.
W ater is my world.
I magining that I have an *Olympic* life.
M eeting proud athletes.
M emorising all my skills.
I ndoors or outdoors.
N ow is the time to show my will.
G oing for *gold!*

Rosie Campbell (9)
Wellfield Middle School, Whitley Bay

The Magpies

T he magpies
H oway the lads
E veryone cheers wildly.

M ikel Merino scores
A wonderful shot.
G oal! Another one.
P eep! Penalty!
I t's smashed over
E ffortless win.
S t James' Park empties.

Fraser Potter (9)
Wellfield Middle School, Whitley Bay

Ice And Embers

Fireballs are hot,
Snowballs are not.
Pile it up a lot,
Build the biggest plot.

Go to the Nether,
Be very clever.
Fight the Wither,
But do not dither.

Go to a mansion,
Get good enchantments.
Sword with a flame?
You might win the game!

Ben Vincent (9)
Wellfield Middle School, Whitley Bay

Mining

Deep, deep down
deep underground,
you never know
what you will find.

It's dark, dark, dark
but that won't stop me,
I'll keep on going,
just you watch me.

Look, look here
at what I found,
I found green emeralds
underground!

Ryan Cain (9)
Wellfield Middle School, Whitley Bay

Kung Fu

Wishy-washy
Wishy-washy
What can you do?
I can teach you martial arts
Do you like Fu Manchu?
He's a kung fu super dude
Like a lion in a very bad mood
His moves are fast
He can knock you out with his foot
If you mess with the Fu, he'll kick your butt.

Grant Steven Milburn (9)
Wellfield Middle School, Whitley Bay

A Minecraft Adventure

M ining in the day,
 I n your diamond armour.
N ether never not on fire,
E nder Dragon firing at you.
C rafting tables,
R iding horses
A nd trading with villagers too.
F arming.
T rophies earned throughout the game.

Thomas Stanley (9)
Wellfield Middle School, Whitley Bay

Untitled

Ice
cold, freezing
like the tusk of a mammoth.

Fire
as hot as the core
flaming blaze
Fire.

Wood
spiky splinters
axe can slice through it like cheese

As tough as steel
Stone is powerful
rigid, smooth
Stone.

James Worsdale (9)
Wellfield Middle School, Whitley Bay

Winter Wonderland

Icy winter wonderland, snowflakes falling all around us.
The pointy, snowy mountain sitting right in front of the frozen sun.
The sound of the crunchy, glittering snow beneath my feet.
Wrapped in my coat and scarf,
Polar bears' fluffy fur hits me when I hike up the mountains.

Dylan Robinson (9)
Wellfield Middle School, Whitley Bay

Mining And Digging

Mining, digging all through the night,
keep a close eye, creepers are in sight.
Find creepers which are out,
don't be their prey
otherwise, you'll not see another day!

Mining, digging all through the night,
keep a close eye, creepers are in sight!

Ava Tierney (10)
Wellfield Middle School, Whitley Bay

Beamish

B eamish is brilliant in all ways.
E xciting place to visit.
A dventure to discover.
M ake your own poster.
I nventions that changed the world.
S team trains that you can ride.
H elpful staff make the perfect visit.

Daniel Browell (10)
Wellfield Middle School, Whitley Bay

Minecraft, The Good And Bad

Creepers coming
to catch me.
Running fast
so I must flee.

Into my house
made of bricks.
Switch on the light
with a fire stick.

Look out my window
I see a mob.
Do I laugh
or do I sob?

Help!

Luke Mennie (9)
Wellfield Middle School, Whitley Bay

Lava

Much coal and iron
and gold to find.
You wonder if you still have time.
Just one more block,
one more, you say,
but an unseen hole
is in your way.
You slip, you fall,
into the lava you go
and burn to a crisp,
all nice and slow...

Olivia Farrington (9)
Wellfield Middle School, Whitley Bay

My Moon

I like to sit on our doorstep
And watch the place above the hill.
I wait for a few minutes
Then the moon appears for me.

Its favourite spot is here,
Because it likes to shine on me.
When it smiles at me
I smile back.
It is my moon.

Carla Filipa Paulino-Goncalves (9)
Wellfield Middle School, Whitley Bay

Animal Farm

A pe, don't act like one of them.
N ewt, it isn't cute.
I guanas have long, crazy beards.
M onkeying around doesn't make me happy.
A lligators are big.
L eopards never change their spots.

Thomas Sidebotham (9)
Wellfield Middle School, Whitley Bay

An Apple A Day

A n apple a day keeps the doctors away
P art of your 5-a-day,
P ips inside that can grow a tree.
L ow calorie,
E specially delicious for a snack.
S o juicy and tasty, you can't beat that!

Sophie Johnson (9)
Wellfield Middle School, Whitley Bay

Fire

F rightened people ran from the burning fire.
I ncredibly, the fire grew bigger and bigger and bigger.
R apidly, the people ran, getting faster and faster.
E xtraordinarily, the fire was caused by a fridge!

Phoebe Olivia Batchelor (9)
Wellfield Middle School, Whitley Bay

Horses!

H orses are cool to ride on,
O n their backs, when you ride them, you put on a saddle,
R iding them is great fun,
S tables are where they live,
E xcited riders raring to go.

Amelia Dodds (9)
Wellfield Middle School, Whitley Bay

Football

Football
Linebacker, quarterback
Hail Mary, screen pass, big hit
Wide recover, linesman, soccer, offside
Red card, goal! Upfront
Winger, strike, step over
Top bins, Rabona
Football.

Max Torre (9)
Wellfield Middle School, Whitley Bay

Quiet And Loud
(A diamante poem)

Quiet
Silence, peaceful
Tiptoe, creeping, whispering
Library, church, soft play, playground
Shouting, banging, screaming
Noisy, deafening,
Loud.

Aimee Cowen (9)
Wellfield Middle School, Whitley Bay

Steve

Here is Steve
he likes to dig
then suddenly
he finds a pig.

He chops it up
into little chunks
cooks it all
then eats it up!

Oliver Stoneman (9)
Wellfield Middle School, Whitley Bay

Once Upon A Crystal

Crystals,
minerals, rocks,
Shining, sparkling, dazzling.
Tetragonal, hexagonal.
Mining, shaping, polishing.
Amethyst, quartz,
diamonds.

Josh Meredith (9)
Wellfield Middle School, Whitley Bay

Football And Rugby
(A diamante poem)

Football
Shoot, boot.
Passing, shooting, scoring.
He ran so fast, his feet were a blur.
Running, rucking, tackling
Rough, tough.
Rugby.

Josh Farrington (9)
Wellfield Middle School, Whitley Bay

What Is It?

It crawls through sewers.
It climbs up drains.
It jumps around corners.
It may be a spider.
Boo!

Ashton Stewart (9)
Wellfield Middle School, Whitley Bay

YoungWriters

YOUNG WRITERS INFORMATION

We hope you have enjoyed reading this book – and that you will continue to in the coming years.

If you're a young writer who enjoys reading and creative writing, or the parent of an enthusiastic poet or story writer, do visit our website **www.youngwriters.co.uk**. Here you will find free competitions, workshops and games, as well as recommended reads, a poetry glossary and our blog.

If you would like to order further copies of this book, or any of our other titles, then please give us a call or visit **www.youngwriters.co.uk**.

Young Writers
Remus House
Coltsfoot Drive
Peterborough
PE2 9BF
(01733) 890066
info@youngwriters.co.uk